I0199130

JACKANAPE AND THE FINGERMEN

JACKANAPE AND THE FINGERMEN

d. harlan wilson

AØP

ANTI-OEDIPUS PRESS

Jackanape and the Fingermen
Copyright © 2021 by D. Harlan Wilson
ISBN: 978-0-99-915356-7
Library of Congress Number: 2021935259
First Hardcover Edition, December 2021

All rights reserved. No part of this book may be reproduced, stored in a retrieval system, or transmitted by any means without the written permission of the author and publisher. Published in the United States by Anti-Oedipus Press, an imprint of Raw Dog Screaming Press.

RAW DOG
SCREAMING
PRESS

www.rawdogscreaming.com

Cover Design by Matthew Revert
www.matthewrevert.com

Anti-Oedipus Press
Grand Rapids, MI

@AntiOedipusP
@antioedipuspress

www.anti-oedipuspress.com

SF
SCHIZ
FLOW

ACKNOWLEDGEMENTS

Gratitude to the editors of *The Café Irreal*, G.S. Evans and Alice Whittenburg, who published *Jackanape* in their seventieth issue (Spring 2019). Some of my earliest stories appeared in this magazine, which is among my foremost inspirations to this day.

Thanks also to Hawgstrüffel Galleria in Reykjavík where *The Fingermen* ran for three months during the summer of 2020 despite a global pandemic. I attended several performances and was taken aback by the scale of the production and the quality of the actors. I will always remain humbled by and grateful for the experience.

"What'll he dress himself in! Gentleman Jack an' his frieze coat."

—Joxer, Seán O'Casey's *Juno and the Paycock*

———●●●———

"I can't remember ever remembering anything. Did I ever remember anything? Or, did we arrive here like epileptics, traveling thorugh the midnight of some unconscious joy?"

—Father, Russell Edson's *The Falling Sickness*

For Njål.

CONTENTS

JACKANAPE

AN OFF-COLOR DISTRACTION

Dramatis

Young Man
Dagny
Brenda
Victim
Bystanders
Detective Johnson
Detective Cork
Old Man
Father
Mother
Boy
Girl
Janitor
Ick
Ink
Irk
Boo Radley

Mise

Vacant interior. Cobalt light.

Each corner of the room converges into a different angle. There is a low-level ceiling with a jagged hole in it, stage left, towards the rear.

Center stage is a freestanding coatrack on which hangs a fedora and a dinner jacket. Clean white rectangles mark the dusty walls where pictures used to be. No windows.

The skin and clothing of the actors are colored in matte shades of gray, as if their bodies have been clipped from an old film noir. The hat and jacket are an irradiated maroon color.

Lights dim on at the beginning and dim out at the end of each scene.

With a few exceptions, all action takes place in this room, in this light.

Scene 1

Long tableaux of the room.

Scene 2
Young Man

A young man in jeans and a collared shirt ambles onstage, pauses, turns and stares blankly at the audience, turns and

*ambles to the coatrack, turns and stares at the audience again,
turns and stares at the coatrack, removes the dinner jacket,
puts his arms in the sleeves, smooths out the lapels, buttons
the jacket, turns to the audience, glances down at the jacket,
glances at the audience, and grins a plastic grin.*

*The coat begins to strangle the man, tightening on his midriff
and closing around his throat, forcing his arms behind his back
in an awkward, anguished pose as he struggles for his life. He
falls down. We hear the sound of bones breaking as the man's
head and limbs pound the floor and he squawks, croaks, and
gurgles in pain. Then he lies still.*

*As the lights dim out, the jacket goes limp, like a boa
constrictor releasing its grip on prey.*

Scene 3
Dagny, Brenda

*Holding hands, a young couple enters stage right. They walk
across the room as if strolling leisurely through a park.*

BRENDA   Isn't Dagny a girl's name? I never heard of a
boy called Dagny. You sort of look like a girl, I
guess. And a boy. What's that called?

DAGNY   Androgynous. I take after the son of Hermes
and Aphrodite.

BRENDA   Who? That doesn't make any sense. My point
is, in certain lights you look like you could
wear a dress. I don't think Dagny is even a
name.

DAGNY   [*unhanding her*] What's it to you, Brenda? I'm
a man and that's my name. [*Notices the
coatrack.*] What's this?

BRENDA   I don't know. It doesn't belong to you, though, so don't touch it. You're always touching things that don't belong to you. [*Hits him playfully.*]

DAGNY   That's not fair. You haven't known me long enough to know what I touch and what I don't touch. [*Touches the jacket.*] What a handsome number. I think I'll try it on for size.

BRENDA   Dagny! You can't do that!

DAGNY   Who's going to stop me, Brenda? You? I'm a man, remember. I was kidding about the gods.

BRENDA   [*restrained*] Just put the hat on, okay?

DAGNY   I intend to put on the hat. A man puts on a jacket first. First the jacket, then the hat. That's the way men work.

BRENDA   [*hysterical*] This is crazy! [*Screams.*]

DAGNY   [*takes* BRENDA *by the shoulders and shakes her*] Calm down! Calm down! Calm down! [*Screams.*]

Tossing BRENDA *aside,* DAGNY *removes the jacket from the coatrack and yanks it on. He makes a satisfied frog-face and is about to speak when the jacket breaks his arms, then forces him to his knees and completely engulfs him, squeezing him to death in one great contraction.* BRENDA *stands there in a daze, knees buckling, head and lips twitching ... She screams again as the lights dim off.*

Scene 4
Victim, Bystanders

Tableaux of a man being strangled by the jacket as a group of bystanders dressed in burial clothing watch in wide-eyed horror, clutching their mouths and pointing at the crime scene.

Scene 5
Detective Johnson, Detective Cork

Two detectives enter, canvas and examine the room. Their guns are drawn and cocked. They don't notice the coatrack.

CORK   What do you think, Johnson?

JOHNSON   Dunno, Cork. Thirty-nine murders in forty-eight hours. And all of them presumably took place right here in this room. It doesn't add up. [*Reflects.*] Goddamn it, it doesn't add up. [*Pause.*] It doesn't add up, I say.

CORK   It's gotta add up to something. Things add up, right? What are the clues again?

JOHNSON   We don't have any clues. Jesus, Cork. Do you ever listen to me? I'm not your wife. How many times do I have to tell you?

CORK   I don't know. I figure if I keep asking, somehow a clue will turn up. I mean, how do we know the murders took place in the vicinity? Doesn't a clue have to tell us that? What do you think, Johnson?

JOHNSON   Put a cork in it. [*Guffaws.*]

CORK   I'm serious. This is serious. Life and death,
        like.

JOHNSON   My ass. If you can't laugh at the dark, you
           shouldn't grin like the Sphinx. Understand?

CORK   No.

JOHNSON   [*eyeballs the hole in the ceiling*] What's this
           bullshit? [*Points gun at the hole.*] Is anybody
           up there? Hey!

The jacket flies off the coatrack, soars across the room, slaps
JOHNSON *in the head, and knocks him over.* CORK *shrieks.*
JOHNSON *staggers to his feet and fires on the jacket, chasing
after it.* CORK *continues to shriek and shoots haphazardly in
every direction.*

   The jacket flies around like a mad bat.

   *Eventually the detectives catch one another in crossfire. They
fall over dead.*

   The jacket flies back to the coatrack and gently hangs on it.

Scene 6

*Brief tableaux. The room is empty, but now a construction
ladder angles down from the hole in the ceiling.*

Scene 7

*The jacket lies on the floor in a clump. Sound of heavy breathing
as the fabric rises and falls, rises and falls.*

Scene 8

*Brief tableaux. The jacket is back on the coatrack, but now the
hat lies on the floor.*

Scene 9
Old Man

*An old man with a long white beard wearing an undershirt,
suspenders, and trousers enters stage right. Manipulating a
cane, he hobbles very slowly across the room to the coatrack,
bends over, emits a loud, painful groan, retrieves the hat, stands
with another, louder groan, hangs the hat on the coatrack,
hobbles across the room, and exits stage left.*

Scene 10
Old Man

The same old man from SCENE 9 *appears in* SCENES 10-13.
*In this scene, he enters stage left, hobbles very slowly to the
coatrack, and puts on the jacket, which strangles him to death.*

OLD MAN   [*dying*] Mother! Help me!

Scene 11
Old Man

*The jacket is back on the coatrack (as it is when the lights
dim on in* SCENES 12 and 13). *The old man enters stage right,
hobbles very slowly to the coatrack, and puts on the jacket,
which strangles him to death.*

OLD MAN   [*dying*] Father! Go to hell!

Scene 12
Old Man

*Trembling, the old man enters from the hole in the ceiling,
climbing down the ladder one precarious rung at a time, with
the cane tucked into an armpit. He hobbles very slowly to the
coatrack and puts on the jacket, which strangles him to death.*

OLD MAN [*dying*] God! Let me be!

Scene 13
Old Man

The old man pushes open a trapdoor in the floor, crawls out of it, hobbles very slowly to the coatrack, removes the jacket, stares at the jacket, stares at the hole in the ceiling, stares at the jacket, and hangs it back up. He removes the hat, inspects it, places it on his head, and makes a face, pinching his wrinkled eyes shut ... Nothing happens. Mumbling in consternation, he removes the hat, drops it on the floor, hobbles very slowly back to the trapdoor, crawls in, and shuts it behind him.

Scene 14
Father, Mother, Boy, Girl

This extended scene concerns a family of middle-aged parents and their young children.

FATHER *wears a button-down shirt, tweed slacks, and black galoshes.* MOTHER *looks like an over-the-hill stripper in a tight, short dress and high heels. A ten-year-old* BOY *and* GIRL *wear school uniforms with ankle boots and socks. They are fraternal twins but look identical; only* GIRL's *pigtails differentiate them.*

FATHER *enters stage right and staggers around the room in bewilderment. He gripes to himself as he regards the ladder and the hole in the ceiling. He kicks the ladder. It falls on him.*

FATHER Mother! Mother! I'm stuck! I'm stuck! Help! Help! Help! Help!

Followed by CHILDREN, MOTHER *rushes into the room, shrieks, and falls down. She continues to shriek as she gets up, scanning the room in horror.*

MOTHER I broke my heel!

CHILDREN *shriek.*

FATHER   [*squirming like a pinned insect*] Achtung, you people! Get this thing off of me! Get it off! I'm immobilized, by God!

MOTHER *and* CHILDREN *scurry to the ladder. Together they lift it so* FATHER *can crawl out.*

FATHER   [*standing*] Holy hell! I wasn't expecting that. Usually I'm ready for anything.

MOTHER   [*limping*] I can't walk right. My heel's broke and they took all my pumps!

FATHER   They took more than our clothes, Mother. They took our furniture. They took our appliances. They took our pictures and our carpet ... They even took the monkey! Boo! Boo Radley, where are you! [*Reflects.*] Goddamn it. They wrecked my ceiling, too, breaking in here. Only things they left behind were my hat, my dinner jacket, and the stick of wood I hang them on. Sons of bitches! [*Picks up hat, slams it on coatrack.*] How the hell am I supposed to eat dinner? There's no food. There's nothing to sit on. There's nothing to eat off!

MOTHER   I had a casserole in the fridge.

FATHER   Casserole? Let's keep our eye on the ball, Mother. The refrigerator is gone. Hence the casserole is gone. It's part of history now. All we have to work with is the residual present and a potentially dangerous future.

MOTHER   [*pacing in an effort to fix her shoe*] This damn heel won't go back into place!

CHILDREN *shriek.*

FATHER   CHILDREN!!!

MOTHER   Stop yelling at them, dear! They love you! They love you so much!

FATHER   Apologies. Extreme circumstances beget extreme behavior.

CHILDREN *run to* FATHER *and hug him.*

FATHER   It will be all right once I get my dinner. Now then. I need a table and chair. I need food. I need satisfaction, is what I need. Achtung!

CHILDREN *scamper offstage.*
   MOTHER *removes her shoe and tries to fix the heel, jerking and tugging on it, grunting as if lifting a heavy rock.* FATHER *creeps up behind her, reaches under her arms, and begins to massage her breasts, sometimes gently, sometimes forcefully. Obsessed with the shoe,* MOTHER *ignores him.*
   When CHILDREN *re-enter,* FATHER *abruptly releases his grip, throwing* MOTHER *off balance. She falls down and continues to struggle with the shoe on the floor.*
   GIRL *drags a lightweight table into the room; behind her,* BOY *drags in a chair.*

CHILDREN   [*seeing* MOTHER] Father!

FATHER   What's wrong? What's the matter? She's my wife! She— [*Notices table and chair.*] Ah! Well done, children. I won't ask where you got them—a good day's work should never be put in question. But the day isn't over. Food!

CHILDREN *scamper away.*

FATHER   [*annoyed*] Goddamn it, Mother. Stop paying so much attention to that thing and arrange this table and chair so I can sit down for dinner.

Frustrated, MOTHER *discards the shoe and breaks into tears.*

FATHER   [*assisting* MOTHER *to her feet*] I'm here, darling. Don't fret. Let me help. [*Removes other shoe and escorts her to the table.*] There you are. I'll be sitting down in no time.

MOTHER   [*sniffling*] I'm sorry, dear. I don't know what's come over me. [*Pushes the table to the center of the room next to the coatrack, then arranges the chair behind it, facing the audience.*] Bon appetite.

FATHER   Let's not get ahead of ourselves. We'll see what the children muster from the kitchen of life. For now ... [*Strides to the table, sits in the chair, and allows* MOTHER *to push him in. Sighs deeply.*] That's more like it. A man needs a proper seat before he can take the bull by the horns and make it into his bitch. [*Laughing,* MOTHER *begins to rub his shoulders.*] That feels good. That feels *right*. All will be well, Mother. Focus on the happy moments. They don't happen often, but I must remember that they do in fact *happen*. Otherwise I become fixated on the monotony

of existence. That fixation produces anxiety.
And anxiety—the root-cause of it, I mean—
always ends in the same place: fear of
the inevitability of death and nothingness.
Fear of the Dark, Mother.

MOTHER   I don't like the Dark.

FATHER   I abhor the Dark.

MOTHER   I don't want to die.

FATHER   Everybody dies. That's life.

MOTHER   I don't want it to hurt.

FATHER   It might hurt. That's an important question.
How much will it hurt? Once I'm gone, it
doesn't matter. But it matters when it's
happening.

MOTHER   Once you're gone, nothing matters. Not even
what happened before you left.

FATHER   [*long pause*] That's a good point ... and not a
happy one. Where's my goddamn dinner! I
hope the children don't forget wine. Punitive
measures may be in order.

MOTHER   [*dreamily*] I could use a glass of wine.

Freeze-frame.
 Tableaux of MOTHER *standing behind* FATHER. *Fists clenched
on the table, he grimaces like an ape. She smiles dumbly with
her head tilted to one side.*
 Punctuated by a clash of brass instruments, an oval of light

momentarily falls on the coatrack, blacking out MOTHER, FATHER, *and the rest of the room.*

Action resumes in slow motion. By degrees, MOTHER'*s hands pick up speed until we return to realtime.* FATHER *remains inert—stone-faced and statuesque.*

> MOTHER   [*squeezing an eye shut*] I have the worst headache. It's killing me.

> FATHER   I don't believe in headaches. In any case, a headache can't kill you. Only the symptom can kill you. Only the dark matter lurking beneath the jigsaw pieces of your skull.

> MOTHER   I don't like dark matter.

> FATHER   I abhor dark matter.

> MOTHER   I don't—

MOTHER *is interrupted by* CHILDREN, *who return with dinner. Panting and disheveled,* BOY *has secured a half-empty bottle of wine,* GIRL *a shabby-looking rotisserie chicken. They circle the room in a frenzy. Shaking, they place the food and drink on the table in front of* FATHER, *cling to* MOTHER, *and await a response.*

FATHER *moves his gaze back and forth between the wine and the chicken, like a jeweler scrutinizing diamonds.*

> FATHER   [*impassive, fixated on chicken*]: Children? [CHILDREN *whimper.*] Children? [*They whimper harder.*] Children, you've done it! You've done it, by God! It's dinnertime!

Elated, MOTHER *hugs* CHILDREN, *admiring them, then they all arrange themselves around the table and sit on the floor.*

FATHER *closes his eyes and bows his head. Everybody follows his lead.*

FATHER   Lord? Please give me everything I want, when I want it, no matter why I want it or who it hurts. Lord? Please kill the interlopers who broke into my house and took my things. And Lord? Please bless Boo Radley. I already miss that hairy son of a bitch. May he be swinging through the jungle of eternity. Amen.

MOTHER   Amen.
CHILDREN

MOTHER *and* CHILDREN *push themselves to their knees so they can peer over the table and watch* FATHER *eat. He tears a drumstick from the chicken, sniffs it, turns it over in his hands, and brings it to his mouth.*

FATHER   Wait. [*Angrily flings drumstick at audience.*] I can't eat this! I'm naked! Mother, I'm naked! Achtung! Achtung!

MOTHER   [*gesticulating*] No you're not! You have your clothes on! I can see them! Look!

BOY   [*terrified*] We can see them, Father!

GIRL   [*desperately*] You're all right, Father!

CHILDREN   [*in unison*] Please, Father, please!

FATHER   Goddamn it, you people! You know what I mean. What's wrong with all of you? This is dinner. A man can't rightly eat dinner without his dinner jacket.

MOTHER   Ah! [*Jumps up, loses balance, and falls down. Jumps back up and scrambles to the coatrack. Exclaims.*] Here it is! [*Removes jacket. Drones.*] Here it is. [*Steps behind* FATHER. *Whispers.*] Here it is.

CHILDREN *dive under the table. Trembling in fear, they clench one another.*

FATHER   [*pushes himself from the table and extends arms*] Right.

MOTHER   [*tentatively*] Are you sure?

FATHER   [*glances over shoulder*] Sure about what?

MOTHER   Well ... technically, you don't need a jacket to eat. In fact, even if you were naked—authentically naked, I mean—you could chew and swallow food. You could drink your drink, too. You could do it all, dear.

FATHER   Authentically naked? Are you kidding me?

MOTHER   I don't know what to do ... Should we put your hat on first?

FATHER   We? Hat? [*Pauses.*] Who wears a hat to the dinner table? It's sacrilegious. It's wrong.

MOTHER   I've seen men eat dinner with hats on. I've seen them!

FATHER   That's enough out of you, Mother. Gimme that damn thing. [*Snatches the jacket.*]

Long freeze-frame.

The action resumes in slow motion as FATHER *puts on the jacket and a wide-eyed* MOTHER *backs further and further away from him. Sound of garbled instruments. Once he has his arms in the sleeves and buttons the jacket, fast-forward to realtime.*

FATHER   [*glances across the room at* MOTHER, *then under the table at* CHILDREN] What's going on? What am I missing? Would you please stop acting like so many weirdos? We're a family. Let's start pretending like we're one.

Slowly, MOTHER *returns to the table and takes her spot on the floor.* CHILDREN *crawl out from underneath the table and take their spots. They all sit cross-legged, heads buried in laps.*

FATHER   That's more like it. Now then. [*Swigs wine from the bottle.*] Disgusting. [*Takes another swig and sets the bottle aside.*] The second sip is always worse. I'll get to the third soon enough. [*Tears off remaining drumstick from chicken and bites into it.*] Ak! [*Makes a face but continues to chew.*] This tastes like my goddamn shoe. It's horrible! [*Takes another bite, chewing with his mouth open.*] I've eaten shitty birds before, but holy hell if this isn't the shittiest. Christ! [*Takes another bite. Continues to eat and talk, using the lapel of the jacket to wipe grease from his mouth.*] It doesn't matter, the taste of food and drink. It's fuel—that's how you have to think about it. If one gives one's taste buds too much leeway, the buds will entirely take over and have the run of the house. It's the same thing that happens to dictators with tiny peckers. In order to compensate for their Great Lack, they conquer the world and turn it into their personal crapper. Do you hear me, children? Taste buds are no different, the greedy whores. Give them an inch and they'll take an ell. Before you know it, all of the troops are dead and you're the size of a goddamn whale! Sons of bitches. If I were half the man that my father was, I'd yank my tongue from my mouth and throw it out the window. That's what I'd do! Nonetheless, I persevere. I may not be my father, but I know how to control myself. Which is more than I can say for my mother. You should have seen her! Her footfalls were like meteor strikes. She would eat an entire rack of lamb in one sitting, supplementing the meat with a loaf of garlic bread and an entire key lime pie for dessert. Nary a vegetable entered the dining room on her watch. She hated fruit, too, and she only drank wine under protest; she blamed her hangovers on the grapes. By God, I miss the old pig. When she read me bedtime stories, I could hear her stomach trying to work things out as the folds of her belly smothered me. Her heart beat like a machine gun. Those limp-dick bones of hers weren't meant to carry so much weight. Let me tell you something. If I were my mother, I—"

A mouthful of chicken flies from FATHER's *mouth as the jacket suddenly, viciously attacks him; the arms coil around his neck like tentacles, snapping the popcorn bones of his arms. Everybody screams.* FATHER *falls sideways from the chair and writhes on the floor. Still screaming,* MOTHER *and* CHILDREN *dash offstage.*

FATHER's *scream weakens and dwindles to a loud gurgle as the jacket tightens its grip and eventually breaks his neck with a deafening, echoic crack.*

Scene 15
Janitor

A tall, muscular, age-weathered man wearing an orange prisoner jumpsuit and ankle chains enters stage right and removes everything from the room—table, chairs, coatrack, hat, ladder, jacket, and corpse. He takes the items offstage one at a time. He puts on the hat before moving the coatrack. He drags the corpse of the father by the ankle. Finally, he returns to the empty room, sweeps it with a giant industrial broom, and exits stage left.

Scene 16

Brief tableaux of the empty room. Offstage, the sound of a windstorm and several exploding bombs. Distant screams. Random throat-clearing.

Scene 17
Ick, Ink, Irk

Stage left, three homunculi slowly crawl into the room. They are naked and hairless. Gills in their necks and ribs. No genitals. They speak to one another as they move around the room in straight lines, turning in different directions when they hit a wall upstage or run out of space downstage.

ICK   My gills aren't working, Ink.

INK   We're not underwater, Ick.

ICK   Oh.

IRK   Where are we, Ink?

ICK   I don't know, Irk. I can't breathe.

INK   And yet you continue to live, Ick.

IRK   And breathe. Look at your chest, Ick. It's
expanding and contracting. Like the universe.

ICK *bends his neck and pushes his chin into the hollow of his clavicle, scrutinizing his chest. He runs into a wall.*

IRK   Watch out, Ick. That's how saber-toothed
tigers went extinct. They kept looking at their
chests and slitting their own throats.

ICK   That's a myth, Irk!

INK   He's right, Irk.

ICK   Saber-toothed tigers died because they ran
out of prey, Irk. Their favorite foods were
horses and buffalo and they ate them until
there weren't any left. This was about nine
million years ago.

INK   You're wrong, Ick. Saber-toothed tigers died
in the Quarternary extinction along with all
of the horses and buffalo they preyed upon.
It either had to do with climate change or
the rise of humanity. People probably killed
them. People kill things.

IRK   Ak!

INK   I know, Irk.

The homunculi crawl around stage for several minutes without a word.

ICK   My gills hurt, Ink. They're all dried out, Irk.

IRK   Gills can't dry out, Ick. They're not grapes.

INK   Anything can dry out, Irk. Don't be ridiculous.

IRK   What about sand? Can sand dry out, Ink?
       What about dry ice? It's already dry, Ink!

ICK   I can hear my heart beating in my chest, Ink. It
       doesn't feel right, Irk. What do I do?

IRK   Try not to go extinct.

Lights flicker to the sound of a loud, telltale heartbeat, then return to normal.

ICK   I don't want to go extinct.

INK   You're not going to go extinct, Ick. Only
       groups of organisms can do that. Your heart
       is fine. When it stops beating, then we'll have
       something to talk about.

IRK   We've got too much to talk about as it is, Ink.
       If nothing else, we'll never get bored.

They crawl around stage for several minutes without a word.

ICK   It feels like something is missing.

INK   Under the anvil of extinction, only memory
       remains.

IRK   Memories are the exhaust fumes of reality,
And in the absence of its residue, reality
doesn't exist.

They crawl.

ICK   Ink?

INK   Yes, Ick?

ICK *makes A choking noise and crumples into himself. Crunch of bone.* IRK *emits a long, peircing screech as* INK *hurriedly crawls offstage.*

Scene 18

Long tableaux of the empty room. Offstage, the quiet sound of a jungle at night.

Scene 19

Long tableaux of the empty room. Offstage, the distant sound of thunder and lightning.

Scene 20

Long tableaux of the empty room. Offstage, a barbershop quartet sings the following lyrics through a gramophone:

Western wind, when will thou blow?
The small rain down can rain.
Christ, if my love were in my arms
and I in my bed again.

As the quartet draws out the word "again," the gramophone needle skips and the lyrics play from the beginning. Repeat

*three times, at which point the quartet finishes "again" and the
needle drags across empty vinyl.*

Scene 21

*Long tableaux of the empty room. Offstage, the sound of dull
surf.*

Scene 22

*Long tableaux of the empty room. Offstage, the sound of a
short circuit.*

Scene 23

Long tableaux of the empty room.

Scene 24

Long tableaux of the empty room.

Scene 25
Boo Radley

*Stage left, a chimpanzee in a t-shirt lopes into the room and
paces back and forth, as if looking for something. He pauses
center stage. Pushing out his neck, he squints and blinks at the
audience. There is a single word on the chest of the t-shirt, BOO,
which is the same irradiated maroon color as the jacket and
hat.*

   *The chimp hoots, grunts, gibbers, and chortles, oscillating
between glee and despair, then falls silent and exits stage right.*

CURTAIN

THE FINGERMEN

A SAVAGE DISRUPTION

Dramatis

Gino
Fritz
Knox
Van
Beryl
Amp
Little Gino
Little Fritz
Little Knox
Little Van
Little Beryl
Little Amp
Waitress
Strippers
Bouncers

Mise

Stage right, a group of six men sit in a half circle that opens to the audience. They are all missing one of their index fingers, and they all wear leisure suits and neckties of a different color. Respectively, GINO, FRITZ, KNOX, VAN, BERYL, and AMP are blue, green, red, yellow, orange, and brown.

Stage left is a red telephone box. It has tinted windows and we can't see inside.

A balcony hangs overhead where children enact episodes from the fingermen's past when they recount them to one another. Sometimes they mirror the action onstage. The children wear the same suits in the same corresponding colors. A spotlight shines on them during enactments; otherwise they linger in darkness.

ACT 1

Lights dim on. Everybody is asleep, slumped over or slouched down in their seats. Several of the fingermen snore peacefully.

AMP   [*snorting awake*] Digitus? [*Discombobulated, he glances around the stage, blinking and fidgeting. His eyes rest on* FRITZ.] Well. It looks like we have a new member. Hello, member. Welcome to the group.

Nobody wakes up.

> AMP   Hello! Hello! Hello! Hello! Hello!

The fingermen irritably awaken. VAN *screams, falls backwards out of his chair. Pause.*

> VAN   [*loudly, supine, gazing upwards*] I had a horrible dream! I dreamt I was Ronald Reagan, but it was 1990 and I never became President of the United States of America. Carter beat me in '81. That was the end of my political career. I had to go back to acting to support my family. My children had grown up. They were all losers, and Ron Jr. got addicted to angel dust. Nancy was devastated. The only parts I could land were in B movies. I didn't even get starring roles. In some of them, I didn't even have lines. I had to make all this schlock just to pay for Ron's rehab. I did a gay porno so we could buy Christmas presents. I—

> KNOX   Drama queen.

> AMP   Well spoken, Knox. Get off the floor and get back in your seat, Van. Christ, you go on and on. Get up now. [VAN *rises, sits.*] Fine. As I was saying, we have a new member. Let's welcome him.

Pause.

> ALL   [*droning*] Welcome, member.

> AMP   Right. [*To* FRITZ.] Tell us about yourself.

FRITZ   Okay. Hi. My name's Fritz. I—

AMP   Take it easy, boy. There'll be plenty of time for you to talk. Let's go around the room and introduce ourselves. Who wants to start? Fellas?

Pause. Tentatively Gino raises his left hand.

AMP   You don't have to raise your goddamn hand, Gino. Go.

GINO   Hi. I'm Gino. [*Nods politely to* FRITZ.] Hi.

Pause.

AMP   Anything else?

GINO   No. [*Pause.*] Yes. [*Pause.*] Like what?

AMP   [*sighs*] Like your missing link. My god.

GINO   Link? [*Pause.*] Oh, right. Sorry. [*Lifts right hand, spreading apart three fingers and a thumb. No index finger—just a nub.*] I used to wear a lotta rings. One time I was washing dishes and a ring slipped off and fell in the garbage disposal. It was my favorite ring. Not much to look at. I got it from a street vendor in Belfast. I grew up in Dublin, but my mom used to take me up north to watch the buildings burn. Ironically, she died in a fire. Not in Ireland, though. She died in Cleveland. She fell asleep in bed smoking a cigar. She smoked Auroras. Smoked 'em her whole life. Thing is, she always fell asleep smoking.

The cigar would just fall out of her mouth and burn a hole in the sheets before smoldering out. I guess if you cheat the Devil too many times, the Devil—

AMP   Being succinct is being the best you can be.

GINO   Sorry. [*Pause.*] I'm sorry.

KNOX   Stop apologizing!

GINO   Okay! Apologies. [*Pause.*] Anyway, my ring fell in the garbage disposal and I reached in there to get the ring out, like. The garbage disposal came alive. Nobody turned it on. I certainly didn't turn it on. I feel like that disposal just didn't like me or something. I feel like it wanted to show me who was Boss. Well, it showed me. [*Brandishes nub.*] It makes me feel like I—

AMP   That's the third time you've said the word feel in a matter of seconds. You know the rules. This is a support group. We're not interested in your feelings. Talk to your therapist about your feelings. I swear to God, without me as moderator, we wouldn't get anywhere. [*Pause.*] Van?

BERYL I have to go to the bathroom, Amp.

AMP   [*irked*] So go. Nobody's stopping you! I don't understand you, Beryl. This isn't a classroom and I'm not a fascist dictator.

KNOX   If you say so.

AMP   I say so! That's what I say! [*Reflects.*] Do whatever you want, Beryl.

BERYL   I will. I was just saying I have to go. I'll wait.

AMP   Why are you making emancipation proclamations about the state of your bladder? Jesus in Limbo. [*Pause.*] Van, go.

VAN   Hi. I'm Van.

ALL   [*droning*] Hi, Van.

AMP   Stop that! We don't need to do that. We all know each other except for Fritz. Tell this guy what happened to you already, Van.

VAN *falls asleep*.

AMP   Van!

VAN   [*jarred*] Hello! [*Pause.*] I can't remember how I lost my finger. Something happened and I got amnesia. I don't remember what happened. Something traumatic, I guess. I barely remember my name half the time, but I bought the biggest van I could find to remind me. It's parked outside. [*Points offstage.*] You'd be surprised how small it is for a big van. They don't make them like they used to. So that's why they call me Van. I'm supposed to talk about my name, right? What are we talking about, Amp?

AMP   Fabulous, Van. Thank you so much. [*Makes a face.*] Jesus, Beryl. You look like you're trying to pick up a blade of grass with your butt cheeks. Would you go to the bathroom? Nobody'll think any less of you if you go. It's a natural function that I personally endorse.

BERYL   [*strained*] Whaddya mean? I'm fine. Nothing's wrong.

KNOX *springs forward, tackles* BERYL, *and pins him to the floor.*

KNOX   [*hysterical*] Go to the bathroom! Go to the bathroom! Go to the bathroom!

BERYL   I'm fine!

KNOX   You're not fine!

BERYL   I am fine!

KNOX   You're not! You're unfine! You're unfine!

AMP   [*standing*] Pope in a pulpit! Knock it off! Boys, pull these weird bastards off of each other! Somebody's gonna get killed!

GINO *and* VAN *get up and pull* KNOX *off of* BERYL. *The children emulate the scuffle.* LITTLE BERYL *slips and falls from the balcony onto the stage.*
    Bewildered, FRITZ *remains seated but alert.* LITTLE BERYL *stands, blinks at the audience, and darts offstage.*

AMP   You're setting a wonderful example for our new member, you sons of bitches. [*To* FRITZ.] They're usually not like this. Really. Usually nobody has to go to the bathroom and everybody behaves like a corpse in the grave.

KNOX   [*under his breath*] If I'm a corpse in the grave,
you're a turd in the hallway.

AMP   What's that you say, Knox?

KNOX   [*sitting*] I didn't say anything, Mr. Moderator,
sir.

AMP   I see. [*Reflects.*] You know, your counterpoint
is stupid. Other than a turd being in a hallway
rather than in a toilet where it belongs, that
was a dumb thing, what you said. [KNOX
stares at AMP *until* AMP *looks away.*] Just get
on with it. Tell Fritz why you're here.

Pause.

KNOX   I went on a date with this girl. She got mad
and bit off my finger. [*Shows the group.*]

Pause.

AMP   Is that all?

KNOX   No.

AMP   Right. Well then; it's my turn.

BERYL   What about me?

The telephone rings. All but FRITZ *stiffen and turn to the booth.
Nobody makes an effort to answer the phone.* FRITZ *cocks his
head and glances around the stage. When the phone stops
ringing, the fingermen resume their conversation.*

AMP   Didn't you have a turn, Beryl? You did.

BERYL   I didn't, Amp. I didn't.

GINO   [*harmonizing*] He didn't.
KNOX
VAN

AMP   No singing! This isn't a cartoon. This is life. Act like real men.

VAN   Real men sing. Same as fake men.

AMP   That's enough. Okay, Beryl. Floor's yours.

BERYL   Can I go to the bathroom first? [AMP *stands defiantly.*] I'm just kidding. I actually don't have to go anymore. I feel good, as far as feelings go.

Long pause. AMP *stares angrily at* BERYL, *who stares back at him, blankly, until he sits.*

BERYL   Hi, Fritz. I'm Beryl. [*Confused.*] Where was I? I don't know what to say. [*Reflects.*] Oh, right. [*Confused.*] What was I saying?

KNOX   You were saying you have difficulty talking to people.

AMP   No helping!

KNOX   We'll be here all day if I don't help! I've heard his dumb story a million times!

AMP   Calm down! Stop yelling!

KNOX   I'm not yelling!

AMP   You're yelling!

KNOX   You're yelling!

AMP   You're right!

KNOX   Okay!

Pause.

AMP   [*together*] Beryl!
KNOX

BERYL   Ak! [*Pause.*] That's right. Knox is right. I have difficulty finding ways to talk to people. [*Reflects.*] It's hard. Once I get talking, I'm okay; I can do it all right. See? [*Points to mouth.*] Finding a way to start talking is my problem. I can never think of a social icebreaker to start things moving. So, a few years ago, I scheduled an appointment with my plastic surgeon and he removed my index finger. Not the middle finger. Not the pinky or the thumb. Definitely not the other finger. What's its name? The one between the little finger and the middle finger. What do they call it?

GINO   [*harmonizing*] The ring finger.
KNOX
VAN

AMP   Hey!

BERYL   That's it! The ring finger. [*Reflects.*] Nobody cares about that finger. The thumb isn't really a finger, and the other two don't matter. The index finger is the thing. It's the centerpiece of any hand, and if you remove the centerpiece, well, it's shocking. I mean, is a hand still a hand without it? That's a philosophical question, but you catch my drift. People don't know how to react when they see it, or rather, when they don't see it. But they always have plenty to say, and they usually want to talk about it. So I hacked off my finger and now I got a built-in icebreaker. Whenever I meet somebody new, I just scratch my nose with my surgically tailored hand. It works. I'm happy.

KNOX   Surgically tailored? Moron.

GINO   If you're happy, what are you doing here?

BERYL   Minding my own business, Gino. That's all.

KNOX   Who the hell has their own plastic surgeon? What are you, the President of the United States of America?

BERYL   Only in my dreams.

VAN   That's my dream!

FRITZ   What do you tell people if they ask what happened, Beryl?

AMP   That's a good question, Fritz. Nobody has ever cared enough to ask it. I'm not particularly interested in the answer, but for formality's sake, let's pretend I am. [*Pause.*] Beryl?

BERYL   [*confused*] What was the question?

AMP   [*reflects*] I forgot.

FRITZ   What do you tell people when they ask what happened to your finger?

BERYL   Not the truth. Never the truth.

KNOX   Middle fingers are as important as index fingers. I'd argue that thumbs are more important than any of them. Prehensility is underrated by default; without a thumb, the art of grasping is a lost cause. Still, there's something to be said for thumblessness. A mutated perch bit off my friend Rex's thumb in Lake Erie. He goes to a meeting on Euclid Avenue. They have a great time, he says. They laugh and get along.

AMP   Nobody laughs and gets along, Knox. Who's the drama queen now?

KNOX   What do you know, Amp? You know dick.

GINO   I know somebody who lost his pinky. The meeting he goes to is bigger than my church congregation. I guess pinkies get lost more than anything else. It's like life. Nobody pays attention to the smaller things, which suffer the most. There's nothing worse than a product of neglect.

AMP   Temper your imaginations, boys. Nobody's going to any other meetings. You know damn well nothing else exists unless I'm there to see it. Which brings me to ... *me.* [*Applause offstage. Confused,* FRITZ *glances over his shoulder.* GINO, KNOX, VAN, *and* BERYL *don't react.*] I lost my finger long before anybody else here. I'm kind of a control subject, as it were. I—

VAN I remember!

AMP Ak!

VAN I remember how I lost my finger. [*Reflects.*] Holy cow!

AMP What is it? You had your turn!

KNOX Let him speak, you son of a bitch!

AMP He always speaks! All of you always speak!

KNOX *stands, points at* AMP *with his missing finger, and sits.*

AMP Goddamn it.

VAN [*eagerly*] I was in my van. I was driving through the mountains. It was getting cold outside. The leaves had fallen off the trees. The sun hung in the sky like a fruit—I could've plucked it if I reached out the window, but I was smoking a cigarette. I didn't want the wind to blow ash all over the interior of the van. I'm good to my van. I treat it like I treat myself. You should see the upholstery on the swivel-chairs. The pattern reminisces the boutique style of the 1960s while gesturing towards some unspoken vogue of the future.

AMP   What is this, a shitty novel? You don't need to set the scene. Nobody cares about context.

GINO   I only read shitty novels. Good novels are terrible.

VAN   There I was, in my van, puffing on Newports.

KNOX   Newports?

VAN   At some point, the smoke got so thick, I couldn't see anymore. The air conditioning blew the smoke all around my head, but I refused to open the window and risk the welfare of my van's interior. I kept going—not once did I let up on the accelerator. I never look back; I always go forward, and I don't stop until the end.

GINO   You sound like a commercial for masculinity.

KNOX   Hardly. Aren't Newports menthol? That's what girls smoke!

AMP   Goddamn it!

VAN   I can't remember where I was going. I do remember that I hadn't reached the end. [*Reflects.*] I may have even sped up, just to stick it to Destiny. No cloud of self-generated, potentially self-annihilating smoke was going to tell me what to do. [*Reflects.*] Hmm.

BERYL   What's wrong?

VAN   [*confused*] That's all I know.

AMP   Oh come on! What about your finger?

VAN   What finger?

AMP   Jesus!

GINO   Did you crash?

VAN   No. Of course I didn't crash! I've never even been in a fender-bender. Eventually I put my cigarette out and the smoke evaporated. I drove through the night and when the sun came up I was in Vegas. I won a lot of money playing the slots and I ate dinner at Margaritaville. Jimmy Buffet was there, but he never sang the restaurant's titular song. He didn't sing any of his own material. He only sang Neil Diamond covers. [*Reflects.*] Jimmy Buffet kind of looks like Neil Diamond. They might be the same person, you know.

AMP   This needs to stop. Neil Diamond looks like my grandfather. When he was younger, he looked like Jim Morrison. At no point did he ever resemble Jimmy Buffet! Jimmy Buffet had blonde hair!

BERYL   His hair was as brown as Neil Diamond's during the Floridays tour in the 1980s. Same style, too.

AMP   Both of their hairstyles changed like the wind. They're entertainers, for Chrissakes! They gotta mix things up! [*Stands.*] You're all crazy! What is this? [*Gesticulates.*] Jimmy Buffet is dead! Neil Diamond is dead! So help me God

and Mary and every lifeless soul in Heaven,
Jim Morrison is dead, dead, dead!!!

LITTLE AMP *falls off the balcony and slams into the stage with a great thud. Startled,* FRITZ *jumps out of his chair.* LITTLE AMP *doesn't move.*

FRITZ   Is he okay? [*To the child*.] Hey, are you okay, young man?

BERYL   That's not a young man. [*Swallows*.] It's fine. Don't pay attention. It's fine.

KNOX   It's not fine. But ignore him anyhow. [*Covertly*.] We're supposed to ignore them. [*Glances up*.]

AMP   That's enough! This is an important meeting! I want order!

KNOX   [*firmly but calmly*] Everybody knows what you want, Amp. Take it easy. Sit down. [*Pause*.] SIT. DOWN.

KNOX *and* AMP *stare each other down. Eventually* AMP *crumbles. As he takes his seat,* LITTLE AMP *reanimates and scurries offstage.*

FRITZ   Geez.

The telephone rings. Everybody turns and looks at the booth.

FRITZ   Should I get that?

AMP   No!

FRITZ   Why? Who is it?

GINO   [*harmonizing*] Nobodyyyyyyyyyyyyy.
KNOX
VAN
BERYL

They stare at the booth until the phone stops ringing, then turn back to each other.

FRITZ   [*sitting*] This doesn't make a lot of sense.

GINO   Maybe not. But it does make nonsense, and you know the old adage: *One never questions nonsense.*

BERYL   That's not true. If something doesn't make sense, I want to know why.

KNOX   Me too. Who doesn't? That's not an old adage. That's a bunch of bullshit. You made that up.

GINO   I've never made anything up in my whole life.

VAN   I don't give a care what makes sense.

KNOX   Hoot. Shit. Rat's ass.

VAN   [*confused*] What?

KNOX   You don't give a *hoot* what makes sense. You don't give a *shit* what makes sense. You don't give a *rat's ass* what makes sense. Those are all okay. You can't not give a *care* what makes sense. That's improper English. Dummy.

BERYL   I agree.

VAN   Well, shit. [*Reflects*.] Hoot, I mean.
[*Confused*.] Rat's ass?

AMP   Are you people finished? What is this,
kindergarten? Can we move on please? [*To*
KNOX, *sarcastically*.] With respect, sir.

KNOX   Don't patronize me, Bossman. I don't care
what we do. I only come here because my
therapist makes me.

GINO   Me too.

Pause.

BERYL   I come here because I'm single. I figure one of
these days a nice lady will show up.

KNOX   You wouldn't know what to do with a nice
lady, little boy.

BERYL   I know what to do with nice ladies! I've
been with plenty of nice ladies. Plus, if one
shows up, we both wouldn't have index
fingers, right? That's two social icebreakers.
That's a double whammy. We'd have all kind
of things to start talking about.

KNOX *lets out a Bronx cheer.*

AMP   [*assertively*] Right. Well then. I'll tell my story
and then we can hear from Fritz. [*To* FRITZ.]
Apologies for the delay. I don't know what's
gotten into everybody.

FRITZ   I don't mind. It's Thursday.

BERYL   Is it?

KNOX   What happens on Thursday?

FRITZ   Nothing. That's the thing.

KNOX   That doesn't make any sense.

GINO   It's nonsense. [*Covertly*.] Don't question it.

AMP   Here's how I lost my finger, Fritz. There was a building in my neighborhood that caught fire. I happened to be on the roof across the street. I saw it go up in flames like a pillar of gunpowder. This was over ten years ago now. I could see people burning in the windows. They were yelling their heads off. I distinctly recall an old man who saw me looking at him. He pointed at me with his mouth open as if I were responsible for his crummy demise. Well, I had to do something. I couldn't just let everybody burn and die. I leapt onto the fire escape and clamored down the stairs ...

On the balcony, the children pretend to catch fire. They scream and cry, muffling AMP's *voice. He tries to continue but it's no use. The children get louder and more hysterical.*

AMP   [*looking up*] You godless freaks! Stop that! Stop burning, I say! [*Bellows*.]

The children fall silent.
    Pause.

KNOX   [*calmly*] She was in the wrong.

GINO   Who?

KNOX   That broad who bit off my finger. It wasn't my fault. It was her fault.

AMP   I'm the middle of a story, goddamn you.

KNOX   I was a perfect gentleman. I followed the rules. She was very attractive. I opened doors, pulled out chairs, complimented her hair and shoes, asked her questions about her life, pretended to be interested in her beliefs and ideas. All of the things you're supposed to do, I did. And I looked good. I had combed my hair, ironed my dinner jacket, and put on Old Spice. Then, during dessert, when I wasn't looking, she grabbed my hand ...

GINO   What were you looking at, Knox?

KNOX   I said I wasn't looking, Gino.

GINO   You had to be looking somewhere. Were your eyes closed? How could you see to eat?

KNOX   Don't be a fool. My eyes were open. My eyes are always open.

AMP   Knox?

KNOX   So she grabbed my hand. Next thing I know, I'm spurting all over the restaurant like an oil well. I still remember the crunching noise her teeth made. Look at this thing. [*Holds up damaged hand.*] All the way to the base knuckle. She had a mouth like a catfish.

BERYL   Did she eat your finger?

AMP   Knox.

KNOX   Eat my finger? What's the matter with you? She wasn't a cannibal. She spit it out. She was crazy. She wasn't insane.

BERYL   What's the difference between crazy and insane? They're both crazy.

GINO   They're both insane, too.

KNOX   Insane is more crazy than crazy. You know what I mean, Gino. So do you, Beryl. Wise up or get lost.

VAN   Why did she do that?

KNOX   [*deadpan*] Do what.

VAN   Bite off your finger. You must have said something.

KNOX   I don't know why she did it. I didn't say anything. [*Reflects.*] She's a woman. Women do things.

GINO   You're a dirty liar. There had to be a motive. You had to have said something, or done something. Maybe you *didn't* do or say something. Ever consider that? Maybe your words and your actions fell short of her expectations.

KNOX   Dirty liar?

AMP   Knox!

KNOX   What is it, Amp, you niggling son of a bitch!

Pause.

AMP   We've all heard this before.

KNOX   No you haven't. I've never said anything more than what I've said before.

AMP   Precisely. [*Reflects.*] And you've said that before.

KNOX   Said what?

AMP   That.

KNOX   What's that? All I said was what I said.

AMP   [*deflated*] Christ on Golgotha. Fine. As I was saying ...

GINO   Can I revise my story? I don't like mine. Knox's is better. It has more pizzazz, like. Getting your finger ground up in a garbage disposal is too cliché. That happens to everybody.

AMP   Gino!

GINO   Let's say, like, I see this building, and it's on fire, and people are burning up and getting really upset, so I'm gonna save the day. I run across the street and—

AMP   [*frenzied*] GINO!!!

KNOX   [*pointing at* AMP *with a thumb*] Now *that's* insane. See the difference? Usually when he opens his mouth, it's just crazy. That right there was insanity.

BERYL   I understand.

GINO   I run across the street and ... [*Reflects.*] What happens next? How do I lose my finger? Do I trip and fall on it? Does it get burned up or something?

VAN   You can't fall on your finger.

BERYL   I've fallen on my finger. I fell on it yesterday. It hurt like a mother.

VAN   Which finger?

BERYL   This one. [*Holds up middle finger of left hand.*] No, this one. [*Holds up ring finger of right hand.*]

KNOX   Bull. I don't believe that for two seconds. Show me.

BERYL *stands and awkwardly tries to fall on his finger. He misses and falls on his hip.*

BERYL   Ak!

LITTLE BERYL *mimics* BERYL. *He slips and falls off the balcony, but he catches himself on the platform, gripping the edge. Hanging there, he cries out for his mother. The fingermen stare up at him like a passing airplane. The other children reach down and pull him up.*

AMP   [*dumbfounded*] This is beyond unacceptable.

KNOX   [*to* BERYL] Try it again. You can do it.

BERYL   [*clutching himself*] My hip! It's broken!

KNOX   You're fine. Get up.

GINO   I think he might actually be hurt. Listen to
him.

As BERYL *moans and fidgets,* KNOX, GINO, *and* VAN *lean
forward and listen intently.*

KNOX   I don't hear anything.

VAN   He's clearly making noises, Knox. He's clearly
hurt.

GINO   I do hear something.

BERYL   Would you stop talking about me please?
Somebody help me up!

Nobody moves.

AMP   [*glaring at the fingermen*] Well? Who will
help him? Hello? [*Pause.*] Hello? [*Pause.*]
Hello! Hello! Hello!

KNOX   That'll do, Herr Direktor.

FRITZ *stands and steps towards* BERYL.

AMP   Not you, Fritz! You're just a neophyte. You
shouldn't have to do any hard work. [*Pause.*]

Serpent in a garden! Doesn't anybody here have any manners? This isn't a zoo. We're not animals.

All at once, KNOX *barks like a dog,* GINO *bleats like a goat, and* VAN *cock-a-doodle-doos like a rooster.*

AMP   Good lord!

BERYL   Help me!

FRITZ *offers a hand to* BERYL *and pulls him to his feet.*

BERYL   Thank you. You are a good, fine man, Mr. Fritz.

KNOX   Yeah, thanks. Try it again, Beryl.

BERYL   I'm not trying anything. I'm barely alive as it is. [*Sits.*] Ak! [*Falls out of chair.*]

AMP   There's no need for melodrama. We're all adults here.

FRITZ   Right. Adults. Not animals.

Again, KNOX *barks like a dog,* GINO *bleats like a goat, and* VAN *cock-a-doodle-doos like a rooster.* BERYL *joins in, mooing like a hobbled cow.*
    The phone rings and silences everybody. The fingermen stare at the booth. BERYL *climbs into his chair.*

FRITZ   Shouldn't somebody get that? Who's calling at this time of day? [*Reflects.*] What time of day is it?

Pause.

BERYL   [*hypnotized*] I know who it is.

AMP   Stop that, Beryl. You don't know who that is.

Long pause.

BERYL   We all know who it is.

AMP   Nobody knows who that is. Nobody knows anything, okay?

Long pause.

BERYL   I'm going to answer the phone.

AMP   You're disoriented, Beryl. Just sit there and relax. You're not yourself.

Long pause.

BERYL   I know who I am, Amp.

AMP   No you goddamn don't.

Pause.

BERYL   [*standing*] I'm going to answer the phone. [*Stepping forward.*] Somebody always answers the phone. It might as well be me.

KNOX   Aren't you supposed to be hurt? You're not even limping.

BERYL *starts limping.*

KNOX   Fake limp! Fake limp!

> BERYL   I'm not faking! [*Ominously*.] I'm answering the phone.

BERYL *limps forward.*

> AMP   Somebody do something. Somebody stop that man.

> KNOX   [*officiously*] He's his own man.

> VAN   [*echoing* KNOX*'s tone*] He's his own man.

Pause.

> GINO   He's a man, anyway.

> GINO   [*harmonizing*] Anywayyyyyyyyyyyy.
> KNOX
> VAN

BERYL *reaches out and clutches the handle of the booth.* LITTLE BERYL *emits a horrified shriek from the balcony.* BERYL *pauses, then opens the door and disappears into the booth. The door closes behind him, the phone stops ringing, and* LITTLE BERYL *collapses and dies.*

INTERMISSION

The lights of the theater remain off throughout this interlude during which play the songs "Margaritaville" by Jimmy Buffet, "Solitary Man" by Neil Diamond, and "Touch Me" by the Doors.
  The actors loosen their neckties as a waitress in a skimpy cocktail dress walks onstage and serves them ice cream. The children in the balcony are served by a little girl in a white sun dress. The audience gets nothing, and if anybody tries to leave the theater, security guards bar their way.

ACT 2

VAN   I take it back. Jimmy Buffet doesn't look anything like Neil Diamond. He doesn't look like Jim Morrison either. He looks like Glen Campbell—now and forever.

INTERMISSION

Glen Campbell's "Galveston" and "Wichita Lineman" play as the waitress returns and serves the fingermen martinis. The children overhead have eaten too much ice cream and fallen asleep, draped over the railing of the balcony.

The fingermen sip the drinks leisurely but with resolve.

Before the end of the second song, the waitress retrieves their empty glasses and exits the stage as the fingermen loosen and tighten their neckties, trying to collect themselves.

ACT 3

KNOX   I'm drunk. I should never drink. I can't handle my liquor.

AMP   [*covertly*] That's not what you're supposed to say, Knox.

KNOX   We're all saying what we're supposed to say, Mein Führer. We can't say anything else. It's impossible.

FRITZ   Where did Beryl go? I'm worried about him. Is he okay?

AMP   You worry a lot if people are okay. Don't worry so much. Everybody's okay. Even when they get killed, they're okay. Okay?

FRITZ   [*distraught*] Is he dead?

AMP   No. Jesus, don't be silly. It's nothing like that. He just answered the phone.

VAN *falls asleep and emits an egregious snore that may or may not be performative.*

KNOX   Fake snore! Fake snore!

VAN   [*snorting awake*] Ak!

KNOX   Fake awakening! Fake awakening! [*Gesticulates.*] He's faking!

AMP   Knox! Control yourself, goddamn it! You're off track, you deranged hobo!

VAN   Why would I fake waking up, let alone snoring?

KNOX   See! If he had been sleeping, he wouldn't know that he was snoring, and he wouldn't know that I called his snore fake. Ha!

AMP   [*covertly*] Give me a break, Knox. Take it easy. This is serious.

GINO   He's right, Amp. Van's faking. He's a little faker.

VAN   I'm not a little faker!

GINO   [*harmonizing*] He's a little faker, don't you
KNOX   know. He's a little faker, watch your dough.

AMP   Fine, he's a faker. Fritz? You were saying.

FRITZ   I was? [*Confused.*] Oh, yes. [*Reflects.*] I was
saying something. We all say things, right?

GINO   There you go, boy. Now you're getting the
hang of it.

KNOX *passes out, falling forward out of his chair.*

AMP   [*in a hushed tone*] Let's reconnoiter, then. I
was telling my story. Where did I leave off?
I was on fire, I think, with one child tucked
beneath each arm. I shielded them from the
flames that were consuming me as I
scrambled to get them outside, but I got
trapped and I had to drop them to punch
through a window ...

KNOX   [*awakening*] I'm up!

AMP   Ak!

KNOX   I feel refreshed. I just needed to sleep that
one off. Thank God for unconsciousness.
[*Cracks neck.*]

GINO   I don't think you slept for more than fifteen
seconds, Knox.

KNOX   I slept plenty. It was a power nap.

GINO   The power nap to end all power naps.

KNOX   Mind your business, Gino.

VAN   I have to go to the bathroom. Am I allowed to
go? What's the prototype? I forgot.

KNOX   Protocol.

VAN   [*confused*] Protocol?

KNOX   Stop trying to use words. [*Pause.*] I need a
Bloody Mary over here!

VAN   [*squirming in chair*] I really have to go. It's
uncomfortable.

KNOX   So go. [*Pause.*] Waitress! Baileys and coffee!

GINO   You just got up. Do you usually drink this
much in the morning?

KNOX   It's not the morning. [*Reflects.*] Is it? [*Reflects.*]
I drink what I drink, is all.

FRITZ   That's what my mother does.

AMP   Gentlemen, please.

KNOX   Gentlemen my ass. Waitress! I'm starting to
shake. I'm getting the DTs. [*Observes hands.*]

AMP   [*deep-voiced*] Delirium tremens.

AMP's *intonation echoes across the theater. The fingermen
glance around dumbly.*

GINO   You got the DTs after one martini? That's bad.
You're a lightweight.

KNOX   You're right. I already admitted that!

VAN   Boy, I really have to go to the bathroom.

KNOX *springs forward, tackles* VAN, *and pins him to the floor.*

> KNOX [*hysterical*] Go to the bathroom! Go to the bathroom! Go to the bathroom!

> VAN I'm fine!

> KNOX You're not fine!

> VAN I am fine!

> KNOX You're not! You're unfine! You're unfine!

> AMP Fire in Hell! Fritz, Gino—do something, goddamn it!

FRITZ *and* GINO *stand and pull* KNOX *off of* VAN. *The children emulate the scuffle. This time, all of them fall from the balcony onto the stage, then scurry offstage.*

> AMP I hate life. [*Reflects.*] Waitress!

> KNOX Waitress! Help us! We're dying of thirst!

The waitress returns with another round of drinks. She serves everybody and exits. AMP, KNOX, *and* GINO *drink them in quick, ravenous gulps.* FRITZ *watches them, then does likewise.*

> KNOX [*burping*] That hit the spot.

GINO *bleats like a goat and* VAN *cock-a-doodle-doos like a rooster.*
  Pause.

> KNOX [*confused*] Where am I?

VAN   I shouldn't have drank that. My bladder was already overfull.

KNOX   [*disoriented*] What's that you say about your bladder?

VAN   Nothing. [*Reflects.*] I didn't say anything.

Pause.

AMP   Right. As I was saying, I dropped the children. They burned up. It was like I dropped two balls of newspaper into a fire. I can still hear their little screams ...

KNOX   What the hell are you talking about, Amp? You killed some children? Son of a bitch.

AMP   You know what I did, Knox.

KNOX   Then why are you talking about it? Why are we talking about anything? [*Confused.*] What is this place? Who are you people?

GINO   You can't go to the bathroom, Van. We're at a meeting. Get it out of your head.

VAN   It's not in my head. There's nothing in my head. I don't even know where the bathroom is. I've never gone before.

KNOX   Horseshit. I've gone to the bathroom with you.

VAN   [*laboring*] That is not true. I have never gone to the bathroom with you before. I only go to the bathroom alone.

KNOX   I was in the bathroom with you last week. You were talking to the toilet attendant when I got there. Remember? We went into adjacent stalls and talked about Amp's anxieties and insecurities while we crapped. Remember?

AMP   [*continuing with story*] My fingers were a mess. What was left of them anyway. There was barely anything. I recall looking in horror at the scorched and shredded nub of my hand. It was more like the window attacked me. My thumb was okay, thank God …

The phone rings.

AMP   [*talking over the phone*] Despite the literal and metaphorical heat of the situation, somehow I was able to find my severed fingers. All four of them. I ran to my personal surgeon's office, and goddamn it, he sewed them back on …

KNOX   Personal surgeon? You too? My ass.

GINO   Everybody has a personal surgeon. [*Reflects.*] Right?

AMP   All but one of them. This one. [*Brandishes fingerless hand.*] "The finger is dead," my surgeon told me. "Let it go," he told me.

The phone stops ringing.

AMP   But I can't let it go. [*Pause.*] I'll never let it go.

The phone rings.

      GINO   I think I know who that might be. Excuse me.
              [*Stands.*]

       AMP   Gino!

      KNOX   Stop yelling! It exacerbates my anxiety! Why
              d'you think I'm such a prick? I got the anxiety.
              [*Shakes.*]

GINO *strides to the phone booth*.

       AMP   Gino!

      KNOX   Ak!

       VAN   Go to the bathroom for me, Gino! I'm dying!

      GINO   I can do that, Van. [*Reflects.*] I can do anything.
              Watch.

       AMP   No!

Without hesitation, GINO *opens the door and steps inside. The
phone stops ringing, and* LITTLE GINO *dies.* KNOX *passes out.
  Long pause.*

      FRITZ   So they're both in there now?

       AMP   [*dazed*] Calm down, Fritz. Where were we?
              [*Confused.*] Where were we!

       VAN   Ak! [*Pause.*] Dunno where we were. [*Reflects.*]
              I was gonna revise my story, I think.

      KNOX   [*awakening*] You already revised it! [*Falls off
              chair.*] Ak!

FRITZ   No, that was Gino.

KNOX   [*from the floor*] What was Gino? Who are
        you? [*Returns to chair.*] Where am I? What is
        this? I'm alive, right?

AMP   [*covertly*] Easy, Knox.

KNOX   Don't you tell me to be easy, Amp! I got the
        anxiety! [*Shakes.*]

FRITZ   Gino revised his story, I meant. Not Van. This
        will only be the first revision for Van.

VAN   He's right.

AMP   What's with all this revision? And plagiarism!
        Since when has this behavior been an
        acceptable form of ontology?

KNOX   Ontology? Thanks, Professor Plum. Keep your
        Big Words to yourself.

AMP   It's not a big word. There's only four syllables
        and one vowel in ontology.

VAN   Three vowels.

AMP   [*confused*] Three vowels? There's one vowel.
        The *o*.

VAN   Yeah, but there's three *o*s in the word, right?
        [*Spells word aloud.*] O-n-t-o-l-o-g-y. [*Reflects.*]
        That's three *o*s, right? Hence three vowels

KNOX   You're goddamn right, Van.

VAN   Right. So, like, there's three. I mean, if you see three people, you don't just say there's one person.

KNOX   Right again. [*To* AMP.] You're an asshole.

AMP   That's not true! Assholery has nothing to do with linguistics.

KNOX   [*posturing*] A professor is one who talks in someone else's sleep.

VAN *and* KNOX *snicker.* FRITZ *smiles.*

AMP   That's not funny. [*Reflects.*] That's not funny! It's plagiarism!

VAN   It's funny.

AMP   [*to* FRITZ] Did you think that was funny? Be serious, now.

FRITZ   I don't laugh much.

AMP   That doesn't answer my question.

FRITZ   Isn't humor the most subjective type of human expression?

AMP   That's another question. Another question doesn't answer my question.

Pause.

FRITZ   Laughter is overrated. [*Reflects.*] Laughter has no valence. It's superfluous. It's residue.

AMP   That's not untrue. Nonetheless my question remains unanswered.

FRITZ   [*confused*] I forgot the question.

KNOX   [*to* VAN] I like this guy. What's his name?

VAN   Fritz, I think. [*To* FRITZ.] Hey Fritz. Wanna hear how I lost my finger?

FRITZ   Yes?

AMP   No!

KNOX   [*singing with an affected lilt*] Yeeeeeeeesssss.

VAN   There I was, at a cockfight, puffing on Newports. My rooster's ego was bigger than the barn he lived in. Chaunticleer had nothing on him, and he had infinitely more wives and whores at his disposal. He was a mean son of a bitch, too. And tough. He beat up a Great Dane, once, just because the thing looked too pretty.

FRITZ   Good allusion to Chaucer. Your story has style.

VAN   Hey, thanks.

KNOX   Horseshit. How the hell did you know if your rooster thought that dog was pretty? Don't even tell me it talked.

VAN   It didn't talk, per se, but it had a speaking voice, like. It communicated with me, like. I understood it.

Pause.

KNOX   I'm gonna kill you if you say something like that again.

AMP   Nobody's killing anybody.

VAN   It's okay. Most of us are already dead.

AMP   Nobody's already dead.

VAN   Okay.

Pause.

FRITZ   Am I dead?

AMP   I just said nobody's dead. That means nobody's dead. Okay?

The fingermen trade perplexed glances.

FRITZ   What's your rooster's name, Van?

VAN   What?

FRITZ   Your rooster. Does it have a name?

VAN   It's dead. I buried it. It's not my rooster anymore. That little devil belongs to God now.

FRITZ   I'm sorry.

VAN   Not a problem. It was just a rooster.

FRITZ   Did it have a name when it was alive?

VAN   [*confused*] Name? [*Reflects.*] It was just a rooster.

FRITZ   Right. Well, what happened? You were revising your story.

VAN   Actually, it's more of a new story than a revision. The only similarity so far is that I was smoking Newports. But I always smoke Newports.

KNOX   You're not smoking Newports right now. I've never seen you smoke a Newport. I've never seen you smoke anything. You don't smoke.

VAN   I smoke. But there's no smoking in here. [*Reflects.*] There's no smoking anywhere.

KNOX   That makes sense.

VAN   Well, it's the truth.

KNOX   It's fiction. Like everything about you.

VAN   What's that supposed to mean?

Pause.

KNOX   You're telling a story, is what I say.

VAN   That's the same thing as telling the truth. Do you want to hear my story or not?

KNOX   Everybody knows how it's gonna end.

VAN   How is that? I don't even know how it ends.

KNOX   The rooster bites your finger off. Or some
        other rooster. Right? You're at a cockfight.

VAN   [*dejected*] Oh.

KNOX *passes out. Long pause.*

AMP   Well, I guess that's it for today. Thanks for
        coming everybody.

VAN   [*to* KNOX] We haven't heard his story yet. [*To*
        FRITZ.] What's your name again?

AMP   You know his name!

VAN   No I don't! I got amnesia! [*Reflects.*] I can't
        even remember what amnesia is! Ak!

KNOX   [*startled awake*] Ak!

AMP   I'm so sorry, Fritz.

FRITZ   It's fine.

KNOX   It's not fine. Nothing is fine. Everything is
        unfine. [*Pause.*] This play is falling apart.

AMP   [*covertly*] This *world*, you mean.

KNOX   World? What world?

AMP   [*covertly*] You know. Don't call it a play, Knox.
        People are watching.

KNOX   People? What people? [*Peers at audience.*]
        Waitress!

VAN *passes out. Almost immediately, he begins to grumble and fidget, harrowed by a bad dream. The fingermen stare listlessly at him.*

VAN   [*awakening*] Nancy! [*Pause.*] Ak!

AMP   [*confused*] Nancy? [*Reflects.*] Why does everybody keep falling asleep?

KNOX   We're drunk, dummy. We're passing out. Plus, we're not people. We're unpeople. We don't act like real people. This is an acausal universe. You have to suspend your disbelief to believe what we do.

AMP   Stop that! [*Intently.*] Would you stop that please?

VAN   I had a horrible dream. This time, I was Jimmy Carter, but I put on a black wig and a suit with padded shoulders, and I told everybody I was Ronald Reagan. I don't know why. Nobody believed that I was either president, let alone myself. I gave a speech about the dangers of angel dust. My wife Rosie was an addict. I called her Nancy in the speech, but everybody knew who I was talking about. I dabbled now and then in angel dust, but I knew how to control myself, and I knew when enough was enough. I couldn't get through to Rosie, though, even after six stints in rehab. She blew through our savings and I had to start making pornographic films to pay my speech writers. I—

KNOX   Boring!

VAN   That's not boring. That's life!

KNOX   [*Reflects.*] Waitress!

AMP   You've had enough, Knox. Go back to sleep.

KNOX   Don't tell me I've had enough. I know when
I've had enough. And I know when enough is
enough.

AMP   Just relax, goddamn it. Jesus on the Mount.

Long pause.

KNOX   Intermission!

INTERMISSION

The lights go red and begin to strobe as "Land of Confusion" by Genesis blares throughout the theater. A stripper pole descends from the rafters. The waitress enters with three scantily clad women who proceed to work the pole and give the fingermen lap dances. KNOX *loves it.* FRITZ *is apathetic, pokerfaced.* VAN *and* AMP *giggle and squirm uncomfortably. Riveted, the children peer down at the spectacle from the balcony.*

   At the end of the song, the lights return to normal and the stripper pole retracts into the ceiling. Exit the waitress and her entourage.

ACT 4

KNOX   [*to* VAN] Now *that's* life.

Pause.

VAN   You only live once.

Pause.

AMP   I've lived at least six lives.

Pause.

FRITZ   I'm not entirely certain that I've ever lived at
all.

Long pause.

KNOX   Let's do another intermission. [*To the
audience.*] Folks, you can go to the bathroom,
if you like.

INTERMISSION

Lights dim off. Sound of snoring and sex.

ACT 5

The phone rings. Lights dim on.
    AMP, KNOX, *and* VAN *sleep soundly.* FRITZ *stands center
stage with arms crossed, watching them intently.*

FRITZ   Hello! [*Pause*.] Ak! [*Pause.*] Hello! [*Pause.*] Ak!
[*Pause.*] Hello! Hello! [*Pause.*] Ak! Ak! Ak! Ak!

AMP, KNOX, *and* VAN *spasm awake.*

KNOX   Ak!

VAN   Ak! Ak!

AMP   Ak! [*Pause.*] Afterlife in the sky! What in God's
name is happening now?

FRITZ   The phone's been ringing for awhile. I feel like I should answer it.

AMP   Goddamn you, Fritz! No feelings aloud!

KNOX   [*to* FRITZ] Haven't you learned anything, boy?

VAN   I'm sick of not being able to have no feelings. I have them! I have them despite the rules.

AMP   Nonetheless. Rules are rules.

KNOX   They're your rules. They don't mean anything.

AMP   They mean everything!

Pause.

FRITZ   The phone's still ringing.

KNOX   We have ears!

FRITZ   [*pivoting*] Why don't I just see who that is.

AMP, KNOX, *and* VAN *scream as loud as they can. So do the children. The phone stops ringing.*

AMP   [*covertly*] Christ, that was a close one. [*To* FRITZ.] Listen, son. Have a seat. The meeting's not over yet. It's only just begun.

KNOX   Begun my ass. I've had it. I'm a hot mess.

VAN   If I don't go to the bathroom …

KNOX *tenses up.*

AMP   Knox! We haven't even established a context yet, you unholy bastard. Fritz still needs to tell us his story. Then, based on our stories, individually and collectively, we need to figure things out.

FRITZ   [*sitting*] Figure things out?

AMP   Right. You know.

KNOX   No he doesn't! Nobody knows what you're talking about. Nobody knows anything!

AMP   Stop that, Knox! Yes, you do know something. We need to figure things out. That's why we're here, right? To understand ourselves. The better we understand ourselves, the better we can cope with our losses. [*Raises fingerless hand.*]

KNOX   Says you. I'm here for the Beelines. With a capital B.

FRITZ   Beelines?

KNOX   Booze. Broads. Banter. [*Pause*]. The Beelines. [*Passes out.*]

VAN   [*clutching his groin*] I can't remember why I'm here. I can't think straight.

The phone rings. AMP, VAN, and the children scream. KNOX wakes up and screams. The phone stops ringing.

VAN   [*breaks into tears*] I can't take it anymore! I'm out of gas.

KNOX   [*groggily*] Out of gas and full of piss.

Pause.

VAN   [*sniffling*] If they call again, I'm answering the phone. I got something to say.

FRITZ   They? Who's calling?

AMP   [*covertly*] That's crazy talk, Van. If you got something to say, say it to the group.

VAN   I've said enough to the group! We're barely a group anymore anyway!

AMP   Baloney. There is only the group, and nothing else. Beyond the margins of the group lies chaos.

KNOX   The group is a joke! Like the cosmos. Like this. [*Shows missing finger.*]

FRITZ   Are Beryl and Gino coming back? What are they doing in there?

AMP   You're hysterical, Fritz. Calm down.

FRITZ   I'm not hysterical. I don't even think I raised my tone of voice. Did I?

Pause.

VAN   Can we just take a break or something? I need to concentrate.

KNOX   Concentrate on not going to the bathroom.

KNOX   You don't have to concentrate on not doing
        something. Just don't do it.

VAN   Easier said than done.

KNOX   No. Easier done than said.

AMP   Okay, boys. Let's keep our eyes on the ball.
        [*Pause.*] Okay, Fritz. Tell us about yourself.

FRITZ   Really? Okay. My name's Fritz. I—

The phone rings. Still clutching himself, VAN *leaps out of his
chair and darts towards the booth, screaming madly. At the
ready,* KNOX *tackles him by the legs and brings him down.* VAN
flails like a stepped-on animal, kicking KNOX *in the head until he
knocks him out, then gets up and scurries into the booth.*
    The phone stops ringing. LITTLE VAN *calls out for his mother
and dies.*

AMP   Oh my God!

FRITZ   [*standing*] Is he okay?

AMP   Of course he's okay! [*Looks at* KNOX *in horror.*]
        Tell us about yourself! Tell us about yourself!

FRITZ   It's only you and me now. There is no us.

KNOX   [*coming to*] Horseshit! [*Confused.*] I'm
        perfectly alive! [*Reflects.*] Ak! [*Dies.*]

LITTLE KNOX *dies. His body falls out of the balcony and lands on*
KNOX.

AMP   Oh my God!

The waitress returns, flanked by two muscled bouncers in black t-shirts and tight jeans. She swaggers to the bodies with a plastic grin. The bouncers pick them up by the ankles and drag them offstage.

The phone rings for two minutes. FRITZ and AMP stare at the booth dreamily until it stops ringing.

FRITZ   Is this normal?

AMP   Perfectly. This always happens.

FRITZ   People dying?

AMP   Sure. People die all the time.

FRITZ   People you know? Right in front of you?

AMP   Don't pay attention to that. That's just, like, theatrics.

FRITZ   So Knox is alive?

AMP   No, he's dead, I think. Very much dead.

FRITZ   That can't be normal.

AMP   You'd be surprised what's normal.

FRITZ   Children falling out of the sky—is that normal, too?

Pause.

AMP   Don't be dramatic. There's no sky up there.

FRITZ *and* AMP *peer upwards. The phone rings and they peer*

*at the booth. Accompanying the rings are garbled bits of music
and tortured, agonized moans.*

> AMP   [*loudly*] Don't mind that. That's just people
>   burning in Hell.

The phone stops ringing.
  Fatigued, AMP *leans over, elbows on knees, hangs his head
and breathes deeply.* FRITZ *paces back and forth, then sits.*

> AMP   [*straightening up*] I was just kidding about
>   Hell. There's no goddamn Hell. Nobody's dead
>   either. I was just kidding about that, too.

> FRITZ   I know. [*Pause.*] What do we do, then?

> AMP   I don't know. [*Pause.*] Tell me about yourself.

> FRITZ   Honestly, I don't like to talk about myself.
>   Talking about myself makes me feel like hell.

> AMP   I understand. [*Pause.*] Tell me about yourself.

> FRITZ   I'd rather not. The idea of being narcissistic
>   makes me cringe.

> AMP   It's not narcissistic to tell me about yourself.

> FRITZ   It feels that way.

> AMP   Not if you don't have feelings, it doesn't.
>   That's why there's no feelings allowed here.

> FRITZ   Pretending you don't have feelings doesn't
>   mean you don't have feelings. Everybody has
>   feelings. Mass murderers have feelings.

AMP   I see. [*Pause.*] Tell me something about yourself and why you're here today.

FRITZ   Honestly, I barely remember why I'm here, let alone who I am.

AMP   That makes sense. I feel that way all the time.

FRITZ   [*confused*] But you're against feelings. You deny feelings. You're altogether anti-feeling.

AMP   Yes. [*Pause.*] For the most part, anyway. [*Pause.*] Being against feelings or in denial of feelings or altogether anti-feeling is mostly just something you say, though. [*Reflects.*] We say a lot of things, after all. I mean, we have to say something, right? [*Long pause.*] Tell me about yourself.

FRITZ   No.

AMP   Please?

FRITZ   It won't sit well with me, if I tell you about myself. I'd rather listen to other people tell me about themselves. I'm a much better listener than a talker. All talk, no matter what it's about, is about yourself.

AMP   I get it. [*Pause.*] I'm all out of breath and all out of material, though. [*Pause.*] It's up to you.

FRITZ   What's up to me?

Pause.

AMP   Telling me about yourself.

Pause.

FRITZ   I don't want to.

Pause.

AMP   You don't have to. By not telling me anything, you tell me something. [*Raises fingerless hand.*]

They stare at the phone booth.

FRITZ   Do you think they'll call again?

AMP   They always call again.

Long pause.

FRITZ   They're not calling.

AMP   They'll call. Wait for it.

Long pause.

FRITZ   Are you drunk?

AMP   I'm no more drunk than I am sober.

Long pause.

FRITZ   Are you alive?

AMP   I'm no more alive than I am—

FRITZ   Dead.

AMP   No.

FRITZ   What then?

Pause.

AMP   I don't know. [*Reflects*.] You know.

Long pause.

FRITZ   Are you you?

AMP   You. Me. What's the difference? To me I'm
me. To somebody else I'm somebody
else. [*Pause.*] Subjectivity. Objectivity. [*Pause.*]
The myth of perception.

Long pause.
  The two remaining children in the balcony begin to cry.

LITTLE AMP   I'm lonely!

LITTLE FRITZ   I'm bored!

AMP   [*harmonizing*] I'm lonelyyyyy. I'm booooored.
FRITZ

The children die.

AMP   That was exciting.

FRITZ   Are they okay?

Pause.

AMP   No.

Pause.

> FRITZ   Are you sure?

Pause.

> AMP   No.

Long pause.

> FRITZ   I wonder if they'll call again.

Pause.

> AMP   They'll probably call again.

Pause.

> FRITZ   Is there a chance they might not call again?
> Did we miss something?

> AMP   Every moment that passes contains an infinite
> number of missed opportunities.

> FRITZ   I know.

Pause.

> AMP   Every moment is an empty shell.

> FRITZ   I know.

Long pause.

> FRITZ   I'm actually getting bored now. I think I'm
> getting lonely, too.

Pause.

        AMP   Wait for it.

Pause.

        FRITZ   Wait for what?

Pause.

        AMP   You know.

Pause.

        FRITZ   I don't know anything. [*Relfects.*] I don't really want to wait for it. I don't really care anymore.

Pause.

        AMP   Nobody cares if you don't care anymore. Concentrate, now.

Pause.

        FRITZ   Concentrate on what?

Pause.

        AMP   The future. [*Pause.*] History. [*Pause.*] The moment.

Long pause.

        FRITZ   It's too much to process. I can't pay attention.

Long pause.

AMP   Don't pay attention. [*Pause.*] Never pay
        attention. [*Pause.*] We are who we aren't, and
        vice versa. [*Pause.*] Here it comes now,
        goddamn it. [*Pause.*] Hold on, Fritz. [*Pause.*]
        You're going to be okay. [*Long pause.*]
        Everybody's going to be okay.

Long pause.
    The phone doesn't ring.
    *Slowly, the door of the phone booth creaks open, casting a
painfully bright light across the stage onto* AMP *and* FRITZ. *We
can't see inside.*
    Tableaux.

CURTAIN

JACKANAPE *and* THE FINGERMEN

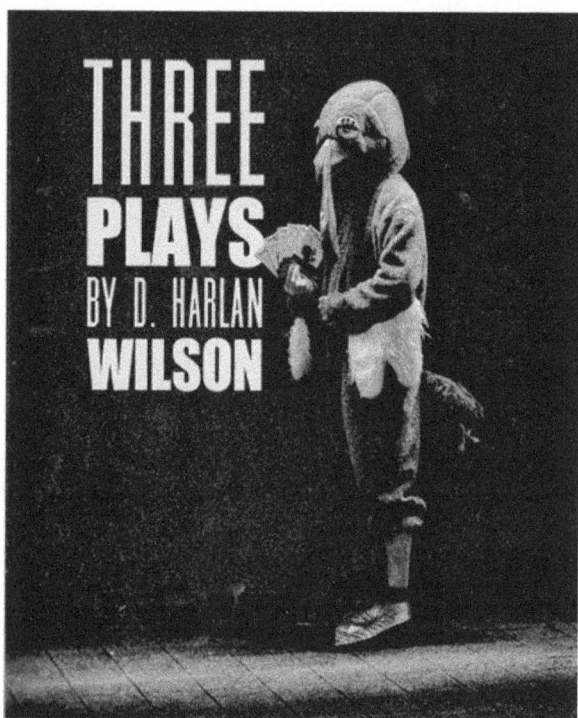

If you enjoyed *Jackanape and the Fingermen*, you may like
D. Harlan Wilson's collection of plays from Black Scat Books.

WWW.BLACKSCATBOOKS.COM

Absurdism, Dada, Surrealism, Pataphysics, Erotica & Works in Translation

BLACK SCAT BOOKS

D. HARLAN WILSON was born in Grand Rapids, Michigan, in 1971. He is an American noveilst, literary critic, playwright, editor, and college professor, with over 30 book-length works of fiction and nonfiction to his name. He holds two M.A. degrees, one in English from University of Massachusetts-Boston, the other in Science Fiction Studies from University of Liverpool; he received his Ph.D. from Michigan State University in 2005. Hundreds of his stories, essays, and reviews have appeared in magazines, journals, and anthologies across the world in multiple languages. His writing has received nominations for and won numerous awards, among them the Locus Award, the Wonderland Book Award, the Pushcart Prize, the Not the Booker Prize, the Big Other Book Award, the Starcherone Innovative Fiction Prize, and others. Wilson lives in Dreamfield, Ohio, with his daughters Maddie and Renee.

www.ingramcontent.com/pod-product-compliance
Lightning Source LLC
Chambersburg PA
CBHW030456100426
42813CB00002B/243